W9-AMN-427

Snap books®

STAR BIOGRAPHIES

Demi Lovato

by Mary Meinking

$7.95

3 4489 00640 5896

CAPSTONE PRESS
a capstone imprint

Snap Books are published by Capstone Press,
1710 Roe Crest Drive, North Mankato, Minnesota 56003
www.capstonepub.com

Copyright © 2013 by Capstone Press, a Capstone imprint.
All rights reserved.
No part of this publication may be reproduced in whole or in part, or stored in a retrieval system,
or transmitted in any form or by any means, electronic, mechanical, photocopying, recording,
or otherwise, without written permission of the publisher.
For information regarding permission, write to Capstone Press,
1710 Roe Crest Drive, North Mankato, Minnesota 56003

Library of Congress Cataloging-in-Publication Data
Meinking, Mary.
  Demi Lovato / by Mary Meinking.
     p. cm. — (Snap books. star biographies)
  Summary: "Describes the life of Demi Lovato, including her musical and acting careers"—Provided by publisher.
  Includes bibliographical references and index.
  ISBN 978-1-4296-8770-6 (library binding)
  ISBN 978-1-4296-9454-4 (paperback)
  ISBN 978-1-62065-350-0 (ebook PDF)
  1. Lovato, Demi, 1992—Juvenile literature. 2. Actors—United States—Biography—Juvenile literature.
  3. Singers—United States—Biography—Juvenile literature. I. Title.

PN2287.L656M46 2013
792.02'8092—dc23
  [B]   2011046829

Editor: Mari Bolte
Designer: Bobbie Nuytten
Media Researcher: Marcie Spence
Production Specialist: Kathy McColley

Photo Credits: Alamy: Allstart Picture Library, 11, Everett Collection, Inc., 24, 29; Corbis: RD/Rob Kim, 23,
Roy Sonobel, 27; Getty Images: Christopher Polk, 6, D Dipasupli, cover, Kelsey McNeal/ABC, 16, Paul Warner,
28, Steve Nesius/Disney Channel, 26; Kobal Collection: Disney Channel, 19, 20, Walt Disney Pictures, 21;
Newscom: BBI/AOJ WENN Photos, 18, David Tonnessen/PacificCoastNews, 13, Deano/Splash News, 17,
John Barrett/Globe-ZUMA, 15, Splash News, 12, ZUMA Press, 5, 9, 10

Essential content terms are **bold** and are defined at the bottom of the page where they first appear.

Printed in the United States of America in North Mankato, Minnesota.
042012   006682CGF12

Table of Contents

CHAPTER 1

Rising Up

It was a warm August night in Los Angeles, California. Celebrities poured into the Hollywood Palladium for VH1's 2011 Do Something Awards. Fans pressed close to catch a glimpse of their favorite stars parading down the blue carpet.

The crowd cheered as 18-year-old Demi Lovato walked past. She was beautiful in a white Burning Torch halter dress with silver details. Her Guiseppe Zanotti platform heels accented the dress. Demi's chocolate brown hair was up in a high ponytail to show off her large silver teardrop earrings. Cocktail rings covered her hands, and rows of silver bangles jingled on her wrists.

Once inside, Demi slipped into the dressing room to change. She was nervous. It had been nearly a year since she had last performed. She freed her hair and slipped on a long Robert Rodriguez dress sparkling with silver birds. As she approached the stage, she heard a fan call, "You're an inspiration, Demi!"

Demi set off her white and silver outfit with Roseark and Loree Rodkin jewelry.

As her music started, Demi emerged onto the foggy stage. She sang her newest song, "Skyscraper," for the first time on TV. As she belted out the final chorus, the platform she was standing on rose into the air. The audience gave her a standing ovation.

The song was from Demi's album *Unbroken*. Its words had a special meaning for her. She had overcome some personal issues, and the song helped inspire her to rise above them.

Demi wasn't just a performer at the Do Something Awards. She was also nominated for two awards.

Unbroken

Demi's third album, *Unbroken*, was released on September 20, 2011. It rocketed to number one on iTunes in only 55 minutes! The online buzz before the album's release helped it become Demi's best-selling album **debut** ever. This album combined **ballads**, pop, and even rap songs. Guest artists included Missy Elliot, Timbaland, Iyaz, and Dev.

Unbroken sold 96,000 copies in its first seven days, making it the number four album that week. Her single "Skyscraper" not only rose from the ground—it rose on the charts too. The song sold more than 176,000 downloads in its first seven days.

"To me, ['Skyscraper'] symbolizes my journey from the person I was to the happy healthy person I am today, and the fact that people are able to rise above anything, despite the odds."

—Demi, in an interview with *Seventeen* magazine

debut: a first showing
ballad: a simple poem that tells a story and is sung

Talent Runs in the Family

On August 20, 1992, a star was born in Dallas, Texas. Her name was Demetria Devonne Lovato, but everyone just called her Demi.

Both of Demi's parents were involved in the entertainment business. Her mom, Dianna Hart, was a Dallas Cowboy cheerleader. Later she became a country music singer. Demi's dad, Patrick Lovato, was in a band. But he quit to be near Demi and her sister Dallas, who was five years older.

Dianna and Patrick divorced in 1994 when Demi was only 2. Patrick moved to New Mexico. Demi and Dallas stayed in Texas with their mom. The following year, Dianna married Eddie de la Garza. Eddie was like a father to the girls. Demi was thrilled when her sister Madison was born in 2002.

Demi is of Hispanic, Italian, and Irish descent.

Like her parents, Demi dreamed of being in the spotlight. She began her career by competing in beauty pageants and talent shows in Texas.

When Demi was 5, her mom took her to **audition** for the TV show *Barney and Friends*. Demi tried out but was turned down because she couldn't read. Over the next year, Demi was determined to become a good reader.

audition: to try out for a performance

With her newfound reading skills, 6-year-old Demi had a second chance to audition for *Barney and Friends*. But she had to choose between the audition and an international pageant. She chose the audition. This time, she was called back.

Demi met her best friend on the show too. She and Selena Gomez were on *Barney and Friends* for two seasons. The two girls were inseparable.

Demi competed in pageants at both the local and state level.

"Everyone who 'makes it' has to deal with the same things: people changing, not being able to trust people. But it's OK because I know I have Selena."

—Demi, in an interview with *People* magazine

Demi and Selena at the Teen Choice Awards in 2011

Demi and Selena, Friends Forever

One hot July day in 1999, 6-year-old Demi stood with her mom in a long line. She was surrounded by 1,400 other kids, all waiting to try out for *Barney and Friends*. Demi turned to the girl next to her and asked if she wanted to color. The girl was Selena Gomez. The two sat on Demi's denim jacket and colored until their names were called.

The girls would go on to star in a movie together. They're good friends to this day.

Offstage

By the time she started middle school, Demi's life wasn't so sweet. As a new student at Cross Timbers Middle School in Colleyville, Texas, she stood out to the other kids. They called her names and even signed a "We Hate Demi" **petition**. The bullying didn't stop.

Demi begged her parents to be homeschooled. Finally they agreed, and Demi was homeschooled from then on. Her favorite subject was math, but she also liked to read. Her favorite books were *The Diary of Anne Frank* and *The Pearl*. She earned her high school diploma in 2009.

Demi tried to feel confident even while being bullied.

petition: a letter signed by many people asking for a change

Demi's performance was a surprise for Carl's family.

Demi Says No to Bullying

In October 2011, Demi co-hosted an anti-bullying rally at the El Capitan Theatre in Hollywood. The rally was held in honor of Carl Joseph Walker-Hoover, a boy who committed suicide in 2009 due to bullying. Demi performed and then asked the crowd to put an end to bullying. "Just know that what you say to someone can [a]ffect them for the rest of their life," Demi Tweeted afterward.

CHAPTER 3

Demi Does It All

After her time on *Barney and Friends* was over, Demi knew she wanted to keep acting. In 2006 she guest-starred on the shows *Prison Break* and *Split Ends*. She got her big break after being cast as Charlotte on the Disney Channel series *As the Bell Rings*.

Acting wasn't the only thing Demi got to do on the show. She also got the chance to sing. Demi had always been a natural musician. She started piano lessons at age 7. A few years later, she began taking singing lessons and learned to play the guitar.

While on *As the Bell Rings*, Demi kept her laptop nearby to write and listen to songs. Her favorite groups were Paramore, Family Force 5, and Alive in Wild Paint. But her role model was Kelly Clarkson. Kelly's musical talent inspired Demi to be come a better singer and songwriter. Demi's hard work paid off. One of Demi's original songs, "Shadow," appeared on the show.

Singing on *As the Bell Rings* would prepare Demi for her future music career.

"I'm literally in love with music. Everything I do in life is for music. If I could, I would marry music."

—Demi, on her Twitter page

Between school, acting, music lessons, and her friends, Demi's days were busy. But she always made time for her family.

"We're like the Brady Bunch because of how close our family is," Demi said. She and her mom, stepdad, and sisters moved from Texas to Los Angeles in 2007. They took trips to Disneyland and hung out, watching Demi's favorite movies.

Demi lived in the guesthouse behind her family's new home. She shared her room with her two dogs, Bailey, a terrier mix, and Bella, a shih tzu.

Demi and her mom are especially close.

Best Birthday

When Demi turned 18, she bought herself a huge present—a house! The $2.25 million Spanish-style house was for her family. It was on a private hillside property in Los Angeles, with a swimming pool and a spa. The pool had a built-in waterfall and a slide. Like in her old home, Demi planned to live in a smaller guesthouse in the backyard. The 820-square-foot (76-square-meter) guesthouse was built over a three-stall garage. It has a kitchen and fireplace.

The main house was built with four bedrooms and 4.5 baths.

Demi needed all that space for herself—her room was full of clothes! Her favorite stores are Urban Outfitters, American Apparel, and Forever-21. Red and black, her favorite colors, dominate her closet. She also loves shoes. She has more than 48 pairs of heels in her closet! Her designers of choice include Christian Louboutin, Prada, and Dolce and Gabbana.

Demi embraces her body's curves and likes to show them off with what she wears. But she also likes to stay in shape. She spends her free time working out and surfing. But she enjoys her favorite snacks—especially pickles, Rice Krispies treats, and chocolate!

One of Demi's favorite hobbies is shopping.

Demi and Joe Jonas sang "This Is Me," a song featured in the soundtrack to *Camp Rock*.

Rocking at Camp

In the summer of 2007, Demi sent in an audition tape for a role in the Disney Channel movie *Camp Rock*. Disney executives were impressed when they heard Demi sing. She landed the lead role of Mitchie Torres, a poor girl trying to make it at music camp. Demi starred alongside Joe Jonas and the teen heartthrob group the Jonas Brothers. Joe played a camp counselor. Kevin and Nick had smaller roles. Demi and the Jo-Bros were instant friends.

Camp Rock made its **premiere** on June 20, 2008. Nearly 9 million viewers tuned in. *Camp Rock* was the second-highest-viewed Disney Channel movie of all time. The movie's popularity helped make Demi Lovato a household name.

The *Camp Rock* soundtrack sold more than 188,000 copies its first week.

In June and July, Demi took her Demi Live! Warm Up Tour on the road. She was promoting her first album, *Don't Forget*. The Jonas Brothers co-wrote and helped produce the album.

From July through September, Demi made guest appearances with Jonas Brothers on their Burnin' Up Tour. Other musicians who joined the tour included Avril Lavigne and Taylor Swift.

Don't Forget was released on September 23, 2008. It reached the number two spot on the Billboard 200 list and sold more than 89,000 copies its first week. Since its release, it has sold more than 500,000 copies in the United States.

Demi toured with the Jonas Brothers several times.

premiere: the first public performance of a film, play, or work of music or dance

Television Princess

Demi continued winning roles on the Disney Channel. She landed the lead role as Sonny Munroe on the TV series *Sonny with a Chance*. The show began airing on February 8, 2009. Demi played a midwestern girl who landed a role in her favorite TV show in Los Angeles. She played this part for two seasons.

Later that year, Demi co-starred with her old friend Selena Gomez in the movie *Princess Protection Program*. Demi played Rosalinda, a princess who was placed in the Princess Protection Program. As part of the program, the princess pretended to be a normal American teen. Selena's character, Carter, was there to help Princess Rosalinda adjust to her new life. *Princess Protection Program* was crowned the third most watched Disney Channel movie with more than 8.5 million viewers.

Multi-Tasker

Demi had become a singer, songwriter, musician, and actress. She made time for her family too. Demi's sisters, Dallas and Madison, had small roles on *Sonny with a Chance*. Madison also made an appearance in *Princess Protection Program*. Demi said, "My life hasn't changed. I've just become busier."

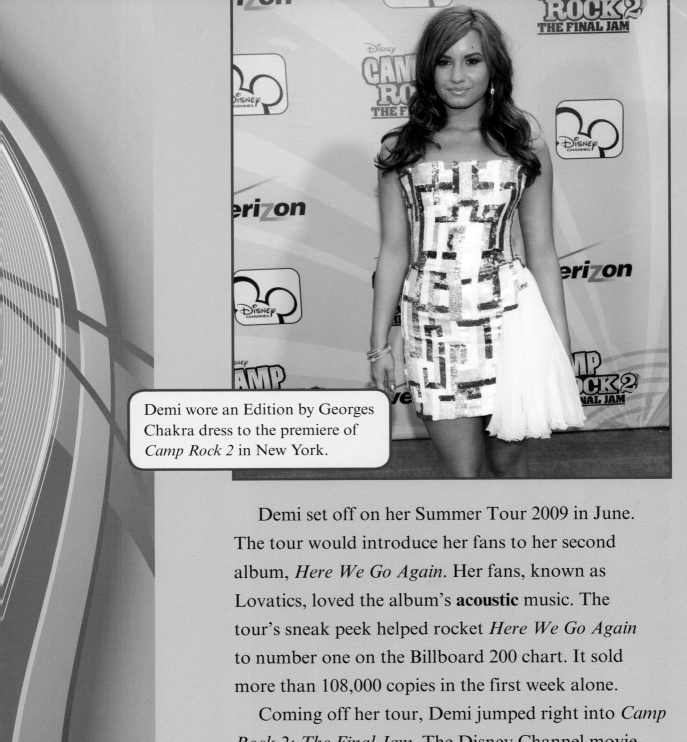

Demi wore an Edition by Georges Chakra dress to the premiere of *Camp Rock 2* in New York.

Demi set off on her Summer Tour 2009 in June. The tour would introduce her fans to her second album, *Here We Go Again*. Her fans, known as Lovatics, loved the album's **acoustic** music. The tour's sneak peek helped rocket *Here We Go Again* to number one on the Billboard 200 chart. It sold more than 108,000 copies in the first week alone.

Coming off her tour, Demi jumped right into *Camp Rock 2: The Final Jam*. The Disney Channel movie premiered September 3, 2010, with more than 8 million viewers. It was the number one cable movie of 2010.

acoustic: music not enhanced by electrical amplification

A Tough Time

The next month Demi joined the Jonas Brothers' Live Concert. She was a special guest in the international tour. But the pressure to be a TV star, hit singer, and Hollywood celeb was too much. She felt pressured to be perfect all the time, both in public and in private.

People photographed Demi wherever she went.

Demi soon left the tour to enter a treatment center. She was treated for physical and emotional issues. She also deleted her Twitter page, later citing mean-spirited comments as the cause. Her 3 million followers were upset at losing their favorite star. The **hashtag** #demicomeback trended throughout the social networking site.

After three months of treatment, Demi was released. She felt like a new person. With her new outlook, Demi decided to focus on her music. Lovatics were thrilled when Demi's third album, *Unbroken*, was released on September 20, 2011. It shot to the top of the iTunes album chart within an hour of its release.

"The journey that I've been on has been very, very difficult over the past few months ... I hope to one day raise awareness of everything so that I can help people too just like you guys helped me through this rough time."

—Demi, to her fans after leaving treatment

hashtag: a way for Twitter users to categorize messages

CHAPTER 5

Giving Back

In 2009, Demi joined her Disney Channel friends in Disney's Friends for Change. Stars who participated included Selena Gomez, Miley Cyrus, and the Jonas Brothers. The stars appeared in commercials that encouraged environmentally-friendly actions. Kids were given the chance to choose how $1 million would be spent on environmental issues. Demi and her Disney friends recorded "Send It On." Proceeds from the song were given to various environmental **charities**. It sold nearly 88,000 tracks in its first two weeks and reached number 20 on Billboard's Hot 100.

In 2010 Friends for Change donated $100,000 to clean up the oil spill in the Gulf of Mexico.

Demi said she felt happier and healthier in 2011.

In April 2011, Demi joined the Jed Foundation's "Love Is Louder Than the Pressure to Be Perfect." The program helped teen girls to accept themselves as they are. As a part of the partnership, Demi became a contributing editor for *Seventeen* magazine. She wrote articles focusing on issues teen girls face. And she wasn't afraid to talk about her own personal issues.

In December Demi was voted one of the top 20 most-involved celebs on Dosomething.org's Web site. Other do-gooder celebs on the list included Lea Michele and Justin Bieber.

charity: a group that raises money or collects goods to help people in need

Future Goals

Demi has been an actress, a musician, and a writer. But her first love is always music. She dreams of going to a school like Berklee College of Music. She hopes to study classical music and improve her guitar skills. She also enjoys writing and would like to write books or movie scripts. Someday she'd even like to try directing a film.

Demi's success has only continued to grow. In 2011 she was named one of the top 10 richest teens in America with a yearly paycheck of $4 million. She ended the year with a small tour called A Special Night with Demi Lovato.

A Special Night with Demi Lovato opened in 10 cities.

Demi began 2012 with a new outlook on life.

Demi planned to kick off a world tour in 2012. She also began working on a new album—one with an urban flair. She hinted at an upcoming song featuring a mystery R&B artist. It's her dream to win a Grammy Award. At her age, she's got plenty of time to win one!

Glossary

acoustic (uh-KOOS-tik)—music not enhanced by electrical amplification; guitars are typically acoustic

audition (aw-DISH-uhn)—to try out for a performance

ballad (BAHL-uhd)—a simple poem that tells a story and is sung

charity (CHAYR-uh-tee)—a group that raises money or collects goods to help people in need

debut (DAY-byoo)—a first showing

hashtag (HASH-tayg)—a way for Twitter users to categorize messages; hashtags are marked with a # symbol

petition (puh-TISH-uhn)—a letter signed by many people asking for a change

premiere (pruh-MIHR)—the first public performance of a film, play, or work of music or dance

Read More

Rajczak, Kristen. *Demi Lovato.* Rising Stars. New York: Gareth Stevens Pub., 2012.

Tieck, Sarah. *Demi Lovato.* Buddy Bios. Edina, Minn.: ABDO Pub. Co., 2010.

Tracy, Kathleen. *Demi Lovato.* A Robbie Reader. Hockessin, Del.: Mitchell Lane Publishers, 2010.

Internet Sites

FactHound offers a safe, fun way to find Internet sites related to this book. All of the sites on FactHound have been researched by our staff.

Here's all you do:

Visit www.facthound.com

Type in this code: 9781429687706

 Check out projects, games and lots more at
www.capstonekids.com

Index